LET US LIVE

A BOOK OF MILLENNIAL VOICES IN POETRY

ERIC REESE

Copyright © 2018 by Eric Reese

All rights reserved.

No part of this book may be reproduced in any form or by any electronic or mechanical means, including information storage and retrieval systems, without written permission from the author, except for the use of brief quotations in a book review.

ISBN: 978-1-925988-37-6

For all the youngsters in a world finding their way!

You have to write the book that wants to be written. And if the book will be too difficult for grown-ups, then you write it for children.

MADELEINE L'ENGLE

CONTENTS

True Love	1
Likes	2
Why her?	3
I'm pregnant	4
Time to move on	5
Time's Blessing	6
No you ain't	7
Sufferage	8
Listen Son!	9
Where's my dad?	10
Virgin no more	11
Life Cycle	12
F4F	13
Depressing	14
Mirrors	15
Do they hear you?	16
True Sweetheart	17
Dream vs Reality	18
A Prom Alone	19
Reflect on this!	20
Where are you?	21
IJS	22
Listen up Trump!	23
Taking Turns	24
Today's Workforce	25
Old vs New	26
I don't look good yet!	27
Food comes first	28

I'm Liked	29
MILF	30
Daddy's gone	31
You are always my baby!	32
Wow!	33
Damn Girl	34
Damn Girl 2	35
Get out my way Bitch	36
Age doesn't cease	37
I want kids, now!	38
Death by a hooker	39
Look Now	40
What do you know!	41
Priceless	42
Partner for Crime	43
Truth indeed	44
Time flies	45
Unforgettable	46
Remember the days	47
Urban Fantasy	48
All for you	49
Love has no age	50

TRUE LOVE

What he always wanted
as a young man
was the love of his parents,
not the money they gave him
to spend on drugs.

LIKES

The attention
she didn't get at home
was received
on the Internet
with each item
that was removed.

WHY HER?

She understood
that she didn't need to change
something about herself
to please the people
in the classroom;

even so,
hated
eating alone
in the recess.

I'M PREGNANT

She took a deep breath
and avoided crying,
despite everything,
she didn't know how
to tell her parents
she was pregnant,
especially
when they thought
she was still a virgin.

TIME TO MOVE ON

Despite being so young,
she understood that
she couldn't compete
with her ex's new girlfriend.

Even better, at least
she got rid of that disaster.

TIME'S BLESSING

The only thing he missed
from youth was the thought
that there would always be
time for everything,
even though it wasn't like that.

NO YOU AIN'T

"Why not?
I'm still young,"
said a granny
while getting
another tattoo.

SUFFERAGE

She regretted saying
she didn't need friends.
Now her boyfriend
cheated on her,
she didn't know
who to talk to about it.

LISTEN SON!

A father looked horrified
when his son began
to make the same mistakes
he had made as a young man.

WHERE'S MY DAD?

During
his entire adolescence,
what he always wanted
was a hug from his father,
but it was difficult
because he didn't even know
who he was.

VIRGIN NO MORE

She had a problem when
she confessed to her lover
that she had lost her virginity
at fourteen when
she was barely seventeen.

LIFE CYCLE

Deep down,
adults hate young people
because they had all the time
that young people now have
and still continue
to do wrong.

F4F

Used to criticize
the half-naked girls
on their social networks
when in the background,
she only wanted
their attention.

DEPRESSING

It was impossible
for them to realize that
their son suffered
from depression,
because apparently,
young people shouldn't
have serious problems.
Unfortunately,
they found him dead
the next morning.

MIRRORS

Sometimes,
he wondered how
he could be a good father
when he hadn't been
the best at being young.

DO THEY HEAR YOU?

He would come home
and say hello to his family,
talk about his day and
everything would be perfect.

Only if his father listened
and his mother stopped
criticizing him.

TRUE SWEETHEART

He was young and successful,
the girls were dying to be with him,
but he preferred to be
with his high school sweetheart.

DREAM VS REALITY

I thought that
when puberty arrived,
I would become a girl
with a magazine body,
not the fat chick
that everyone
made fun of in class.

A PROM ALONE

She watched how
her friends went to the prom
while she complained
about becoming a teen mother.
At least, she dances
with a man between her arms,
while he is asleep.

REFLECT ON THIS!

Looking at the photos
and wanting to be young again,
at least now he knows
what he had to do
to avoid bankruptcy.

WHERE ARE YOU?

They were a lost generation,
in spite of that,
they were already trying
as adults
not to be forgotten.

IJS

Youths were always the ones
who perished in the war
while the adults
turned their backs on them.

LISTEN UP TRUMP!

There could be no hope
if elders keep calling
the young people 'crazy'
instead of 'dreamers'.

TAKING TURNS

Harry was afraid
of his son.
He was learning
while Harry grew old
and prepared to die.

TODAY'S WORKFORCE

Over time,
new always replaces the old,
so the company's elders
feared the arrival
of the young engineer.
That entrepreneurial smile
was going to be their end.

OLD VS NEW

She just wanted
to grow up
and finish school
while her family preferred
that she get married
and have children
as early as possible.

I DON'T LOOK GOOD YET!

He looked himself at the mirror,
trying to find some sign of fat,
for the others he was just bones;
for him, he still believed
that should lose more weight.

FOOD COMES FIRST

Jose had left in the
middle of high school
to start working,
he didn't really care much,
helping his siblings
was more important.

I'M LIKED

Youth passed
before her eyes
while she waited
for the next "like"
on the picture.

MILF

He rejected her
because he was too young
to be with her;
he regretted it
when he was old enough,
but she was already gone.

DADDY'S GONE

If I could go back in time,
I would tell my father
not to take the left,
but the right,
maybe that way
he would still be with me.

YOU ARE ALWAYS MY BABY!

The downside
of being young
is that your opinions
are never worthy
for the adult audience,
no matter how
right you are.

WOW!

I am still young,
but someone older
is healthier than me.

DAMN GIRL

He sought to regain
his joviality
through
the youthful body
of his lover.

DAMN GIRL 2

She was young
and beautiful,
all men wanted her,
and that
drove her husband crazy,
that's why now
he holds her captive
in the house.

GET OUT MY WAY BITCH

Laina didn't care
if they called her crazy,
she would kill
every young woman
she saw
in order to maintain
her beauty.

AGE DOESN'T CEASE

She thought that youth
was in every surgery,
when in reality,
that was something
from only inside.

I WANT KIDS, NOW!

When I was young
I detested children,
now, when I could
no longer have them,
it was what I most desired
for happiness.

DEATH BY A HOOKER

> If he had known
> that he would die
> from an overdose,
> he would have told
> his version of the past
> to stay away
> from that hooker.

LOOK NOW

When Betty was young,
she was the center of attention
for all the boys in school,
but as she got older,
she discovered that
they had only adored her
because of the beauty
and not because of
how smart she was.

WHAT DO YOU KNOW!

During his childhood,
he hated her so much.
Now when he wanted to love,
time had simply run out.

PRICELESS

Sometimes
I envied my grandparents;
they looked like dolls
when I preferred to see myself
as a complete mannequin.

PARTNER FOR CRIME

It wasn't necessary
to remember the mistakes
he made during his youth;
that's what his partner was for,
and she made sure that
she always reminded him of them.

TRUTH INDEED

He had so much he wanted
to share with his children,
but then he remembered
that they had grown up
and if he wasn't for them
when they were young,
they wouldn't be for him now.

TIME FLIES

She turned off the stove
while starting to cry,
remembering
when she was a girl
who dreamed of being a chef;
now she only cooks
for her husband and children.

UNFORGETTABLE

She could love her mother
very much;
but couldn't forgive her
for having made her
lose a lot of her youth
working instead of
sending her to school.

REMEMBER THE DAYS

She missed when
she had no wrinkles,
at least then,
her husband
was still with her.

URBAN FANTASY

> Since he couldn't
> be young forever,
> he preferred to die at nineteen,
> so at least he would look good
> inside his coffin.

ALL FOR YOU

She spent all her youth
wanting to overcome
her rival in love,
and forgot that
although she had finished
being the best,
he still preferred her.

LOVE HAS NO AGE

The other people
looked at them horrified,
but the octogenarian
couple didn't mind
kissing in the rain,
they just wanted to remember
when they were fifteen
and they just met.

www.ingramcontent.com/pod-product-compliance
Lightning Source LLC
Chambersburg PA
CBHW021124080526
44587CB00010B/627